Gnashing at the Gate

An Illustrated Exploration of Horror in Haiku

Danh Chantachak

BookLeaf
Publishing

India | USA | UK

Acknowledgement

Sincere gratitude to the good people at Alvira Publishing for creating the opportunity for writers to challenge themselves. The completion of this project could not have been accomplished without their support.

Of course, I never would have taken on this challenge without the loving support and beautiful illustrations of my partner, Paulina. You always inspire me to be better than I think I can be.

Preface

The poems in this book are inspired by iconic horror scenes from movies, books, and folklore from all over the world, across generations. While the imagery contained within this book may be horrific in nature, perhaps beauty can be gleaned from the purity of its expression.

Darkness and light. Death and life. Evil and good. One cannot exist without the other. Can the same be said of horror and beauty? Let us find out together.

Dedication

This book is dedicated to misunderstood nightmares.

Gnashing at the Gate: An Illustrated Exploration of
Horror in Haiku

© 2021 Danh Chantachak

Presentation by *BookLeaf Publishing*

Web: www.bookleafpub.com

E-mail: info@bookleafpub.com

ISBN: 9789358738940

First edition 2021

1.

Gnashing at the gate

The hounds grow ever-hungry

They can smell your fear

2.

Darkness shrouds his face

The man who walks in shadow

Bloody are his hands

3.

Crows circle above

The earth is heavy with worms

And I stand between

4.

A scream pierces night

Rapid footsteps on pavement

A last breath is drawn

5.

Lightning fractures sky

A glimpse of jagged towers

Dark magic lives here

6.

The crack between doors

Darkness beckons closer look

Something stirs behind

7.

Pale as winter snow

Dead eyes and a wretched smile

She comes for my soul

8.

Blood is on the air

The floor is sticky with it

People turned to meat

9.

Forked tongue, dripping fangs

An ancient wyrm rears its head

I ready my sword

10.

Unstoppable force

Driven by grim savagery

None of us are safe

11.

The vacuum of space

Devoid of sound, air, mercy

Black Leviathan

11

The vacuum of space

12.

Flames dance across skin

His hair is a manic blaze

The man on fire

13.

The final girl runs

Crawling, fighting, being smart

Can she escape fate?

14.

A ruined hellscape

Littered with bones and ashes

Only Death remains

15.

Into the sewer

A slime covered labyrinth

Where hungry eyes watch

16.

Bride of the Devil

The witch steals children from home

To break bread with Him

17.

Bodies in the lake

Bloated and swollen corpses

Drifting with the breeze

18.

Behind charming smile

There lurks a dark passenger

Who hungers for blood

19.

The titan lumbers

Causing death and destruction

World-ender of old

20.

Closets full of bones

Each room bears dark history

And subtle whispers